"In Pawning My Sins, we see Michael Joseph Arcangelini as a drunk, an outlaw, a hedonist, a voyeur, in recovery, opposed to and flowing with shades of modern anxiety, and, most importantly, as a poet. As we read on we find our own relation to these memories, memories of the venal sins we commit in the process of truly living. In this cycle of poems we find Arcangelini fearless with his sins. He stands with them embracing the grace found on the edge of his expanding timeline."

- Jason Baldinger author of *a history of backroads misplaced: selected poems 2010-2020.*

"In *Pawning My Sins*, Michael Joe Arcangelini presents an eclectic collection of poems that fit no single mold. A cross-section of a life, it holds memories from his youth, responses to the pandemic, reflections about the death of his parents. The poems speak about detox and death, elephants in every room and the magic of fireflies. They ask "How do a hummingbird's wings/ sound to the hummingbird?" and imagine "some uncertain future/where words might yet be allowed/to carry untrammeled truth."

- Agnes Vojta, author of *A Coracle for Dreams*

"Michael J. Arcangelini is one of this century's truly gifted poets. His ideas and visions are clear and real and he is one well-crafted poet. His new book, *Pawning My Sins*, is--in Arcangelini's usual fashion–striking, intensely personal, and, at the same time, accessible. These are lived experiences which explore lingering dreams and Detox, Confession and Sweet Coffee Mornings. These poems are on an exploration of Self, all our Selves, and a journey we can make to Truth and Heart. You'll want to join this poet on this particular time away. You'll return an awed and insightful human being."

- Martina Reisz Newberry, author of *Blues for French Roast with Chicory* and *Glyphs*

"MJ Arcangelini tells us he's pawning his sins but quickly reminds us he's having a hard time finding any takers, letting us know that each one is an "elephant in every room" before taking us on a harrowing whirlwind road trip through both the counterculture of the late 20th century, and the journey to come to terms with addiction, sexuality, and the legacy those things carry through the absurdity of pandemics and the rest of the 21st Century. The poems here are breathtaking, heartbreaking, and ultimately lead us through the natural beauty that the poet sees reflected in his own life, and into a broken wise magic that only a poet of MJ Arcangelini's skill can conjure."

- Paul Corman-Roberts, founder of Oakland's annual Beast Crawl poetry festival and author of *Bone Moon Palace* and *We Shoot Typewriters*

PAWNING MY SINS

Poems by M. J. Arcangelini

Luchador Press
Big Tuna, TX

Copyright © M.J. Arcangelini, 2022

First Edition: 1 3 5 7 9 10 8 6 4 2

ISBN: 978-1-958182-09-3

LCCN: 2022940188

Author photo: Jeffrey Braverman

Acknowledgments:

A big thank you to the editors of the following publications where some of these poems previously appeared in one form or another:

Alien Buddha Zine – "How to Play Dead in a Pandemic," "Grief Is a Strange Critter," "In a Shower of Meteors," "The Black Hood," "Lucky Boys," *As It Ought To Be Magazine* – "Ten Movies," "Some Random Thoughts," "An Elephant In Every Room," "The Relative Sanctity of Objects," *Cajun Mutt* – "Outlaw Days (as Outlaw Ghazal)," *The Ekphrastic Review* – "Thoughts on Abandoned Books," *Gasconade Review* – "Bobcat," "My Father Goes to Florida," "Hummingbird at the Bottlebrush," "Afterlife," *Heroin Love Songs* – "Before I Wake," *Live Nude Poems* – "An Absence of Snow," "Lightning Within," "At Raquette Lake," "His Fringe Jacket," *Madness Muse Press* – "Hitchhiker," "Wasted Days," *Necro* – "Death stalking," *North of Oxford* – "Magic," "On the Trail," "Snapshots from a Pandemic (as Pandemic Ghazal)," "Endsheet," *Right Hand Pointing* – "Holy Card," *River Dog* - "The Firm Grip of the Dead, "Angels Don't Hear Confessions," "Sweet Coffee Mornings," *Rusty Truck* – "Lost At Sea," "The Cook After Closing," *Rye Whisky Review* – "Brand Loyalty," "First Night in Detox," *San Francisco Public Library Poem of the Day* – "Working from Home," *Sparkle & Blink 108* – "They Call It Family Law (as Family Law Ghazal)," *Trailer Park Quarterly* – "Shauna Dies Repeatedly," *Voice Lux Journal* – "Dissatisfaction," "Satisfaction," *WineDrunk SideWalk* – "Hour of the Wolf"

TABLE OF CONTENTS

Part I: Pawning my sins

Part II: Sleeping with fireflies

Part III: Snapshots from a pandemic

Part IV: Death stalking

Part V: The old fart takes a header

To Marcus Borgman

*"The Truth? Whatever helps us live
and be strong is the truth.*

- Robinson Jeffers,
  Such Counsels You Gave To Me

PART I

Pawning my sins

PAWNING MY SINS

I took my sins to the pawn shop.
The broker behind the steel bars
                        was unimpressed.
Nothing extraordinary enough to
            stifle his yawn.
Garden variety cruelty to cats and dogs,
spurned lovers, known and unknown,
indifference to blood family.
I trotted out my years of drug abuse,
drug dealing, and
                        24 hour drunkenness.
He said he had to take a discount on that
because the 32 years of sobriety since
were longer than all my periods
of substance abuse added together.

I figured sex would be the clincher,
my ace in the hole,
the thing that would put some
            real money in my pocket.
I laid out on the counter the bathhouse orgies,
anonymous blowjobs in dark bushes,
and the internet hookups
            I've come to depend on to prop up
            an ego sagging as sadly as my butt.

He shook his head indulgently,
pointed to a glass case where the
really expensive sins were displayed

like heirloom jewelry:
incest, rape, animal torture,
violence of all types and degrees,
conning grandmothers out of their
            dead husband's pensions,
political corruption and betrayal,
necrophilia,
            matricide.

He shrugged at me as though to say,
Mister, you just can't compete with this.
In the end he gave me barely enough
to buy dinner in a decent restaurant
and placed my sins on a shelf near the back.

They'll be here, he said, *whenever*
you decide to redeem them.
They may wind up being
                more valuable
to you than you think they are.
Just wait and see who
            you are without them
            and how you feel
about being that person.

Then get back to me.

ANGELS DON'T HEAR CONFESSIONS

Angels are stealth and don't hear confessions – Mike James

Rain falls in the night striking desiccated earth, hesitant
To absorb it; water rolls downhill in rivulets and streams.

Out of the dark, the sound of an engine struggling to make
A three-point turn on an unforgiving country road.

The old house wheezes to breathe, airways clogged
With the solitary occupant's accumulated possessions.

Owls and angels conspire in the stone alcoves of the
Night, rejecting insincere tithes of guilt and regret.

Is that a song the great horned owl offers to the darkness?
Or conversation? This basso of birds rouses sorrow's ghosts.

Promise what you will, the angels won't hear your confession,
They're not there to absolve your sins. Ask the owls for that.

DREAMS LINGER

bright red soaking across
white cotton sheets

the original wound unseen,
ill remembered, forgotten

lost in the fog of waking
staining the rest of the day

with sourceless melancholy
and tinges of dread

TIME PASSING

Late into my seventh decade
time seems to be running
a country mile in
a New York minute,
racing through my
dwindling days.

Acceleration blurs my vision.
Everything looks like
telephone poles
outside the passenger
window of a speeding car.

When I turn to see who's
driving I find I don't know
who, or what, it is.

My pleas to slow down are
useless. In response the
driver turns toward me,
twists its mouth into a
ghoulish, gap-toothed grin
and laughs, spittle flying
into my face on the blast
of hot air shooting through
the wide open window.

AN ELEPHANT IN EVERY ROOM

Different elephants in every room,
occasionally trumpeting to each other with
full throated roars, solicitous quiet plaints.
Swatting metaphoric flies with their tails.
Trunks like alien beings searching for water,
for straw; tusks snagging on the furniture.

I squeeze past them when moving from
room to room, making myself
smaller to avoid direct contact.
I gather their droppings for the
compost pile with a coal shovel,
wondering who keeps feeding them.

There is no one here with whom
to avoid talking about them.
So I creep around by myself,
taking any excuse to go outside.
Hoping that someday Tarzan will yodel
from a nearby tree and lead them all away.

HITCHHIKER

They claim the highway has no best friend.

– Scott Wannberg

Rain constant, as day gives abrupt control to night. An
    offer of
food and a dry bed. The highway still there in the
    morning.

An intersection without gas station, market, or bar.
    Harmonica
in hand, I know 2 songs. No one around to hear for
    hours.

A night and a day at Raquette Lake, the Adirondacks
        unfolding.
Goodbyes past the thruway toll booth before the trooper
        stopped.

In Santa Barbara he goes 3 blocks out of his way to find
        an unoccupied
spot to drop me off. A miracle van whisked me away.

All the windows down, my head hanging out one of them.
My traveling companion and the driver laugh about
        the gun.

AT RAQUETTE LAKE (1973)

For Bette

Fireworks seemed like a great idea to
Celebrate our new-found friendship;
The 20 year old hitchhiker and
The middle-aged birthday girl.
She had some stashed at the cabin.
The moon disassembled and reassembled
Itself on the surface of the lake as we
Approached with the recovered fireworks
And the remaining half of a half-gallon of vodka.
She lit the wicks in turn and then jumped back.
There was the sizzle, then the fizzle as
Each one hissed at our disappointment.
We left them, useless, near the dock, and set out
To peek into the windows of
Unoccupied neighboring cabins
To critique their interior design.
The bottle going back and forth,
While we passed the cool night with
Gossip, giggles, and secrets revealed.
As morning eased into the landscape
The lake emitted a blanketing mist which
Crawled across the yards, a persistent
Nudge sending us at last to our separate beds.

OUTLAW DAYS

Reaching arms into the air in the middle of winter
to speculate angles of light in summer and fall.

Dirt bikes along mud trails. Hauling sacks of soil and
  mulch
to holes dug deep through the snow. Wide and waiting.

Grasshopper infestations. Rodents gnaw bark, ringing the
  bases.
Deer navigating drought eat succulent leaves, lucrative buds.

Diving into blackberries when a helicopter from the river
  canyon
rises above the trees, flies low over the garden. That wind.

He told me to shoot anyone I caught in the patch.
Over their heads? I ventured. No, he said, shoot them.

Some drove up from LA to dicker over prices. Negotiations
grow tense. Lines and shots into the night. No fuckin' sale.

THEY CALL IT FAMILY LAW

While paying lawyers to negotiate the swap of a CD for
some potted plants, he says: *It's the principle of the thing.*

What was he doing bathing his three year old daughter?
The same story told in different ways.

She didn't want half his fishing boat until the lawyer told
her she could get it. Community property state of mind.

She kept a secret diary of all his transgressions,
then pounded him with them like a hail storm.

The lawyer said: *The office bank balance is anemic. Find
someone with money in retainer and do something billable.*

After the custody/visitation decision and doing time for DUIs,
he hunkered into a sleeping bag with his freshly serviced
    revolver.

MEETING KATIE

(San Francisco, 1977)

The only person I knew at the party was the
girl who brought me and she disappeared into it.

A pretty blond was standing in the middle of the
crowded kitchen, head bowed, quietly crying.

She appeared haphazard, like someone else dressed her.
I'd had just enough to drink that I walked over.

She turned her weeping eyes to mine for a moment then
laid her head on my shoulder. I held her, shaking.

At the time I thought that having a woman was a good idea.
We started dating. I never found out why she was crying.

DATING KATIE

(San Francisco, 1977)

I lived in a seedy hotel among the North Beach strip joints.
A trained dancer, she made sex a sublime *pas de deux*, even
    there.

One day we were hanging at the bar where I worked when
Dean Martin's first wife took a polaroid of us together, laughing.

In Sausalito we crashed a wedding party at the No Name Bar.
I wanted to leave, but Katie said "Just act like you belong."

At the Condor Club strip joint one afternoon, I paid street
Prices so she could see if Carol Doda could actually dance.

While driving to an east bay suburb she told me that she knew
D. A. Pennebaker. Her attitude said I was insufficiently
    impressed.

She announced to me that I did not love her. I didn't know
If I loved her or not, but at that moment I didn't even like her.

And that was it. We didn't hang out in the same places.
I never saw her again. I never knew if I'd made her cry.

HIS FRINGE JACKET (1972)

He figured he was at least
half in love with her, most likely
the half usually labeled lust.
He was so in love with her
that he gave her his tan leather
jacket with the long fringe.
He wore that jacket everywhere,
even when the Ohio summer was
too hot and humid for leather.
He liked the way it made him feel,
the weight of it, the way he imagined
he looked wearing it at a rock concert.
So when he gave it to her, because
she told him how much she liked it,
it was like giving her a dozen roses and
a 2 pound box of Whitman chocolates.
She liked it so much that she
took it with her when she moved to
the West Coast with her boyfriend.
After she left he appeared diminished.
In Oregon she soon tired of the jacket,
which never really fit, and gave it
to someone she'd just met.

ONE HOT AFTERNOON

1.

in the clinic parking lot
she fires up a cigarette
leaning against the tailgate
of her SUV
short-shorts riding high
on her ample thighs
her right knee shaking
bouncing up and down
urgently
as she exhales clouds
of toxins to mix with the
fumes rising from the searing
asphalt of a hot day
then she tosses the butt end
to the pavement, finished,
grinds it out with the toes
of her flip-flop clad foot
and walks inside
to see her doctor

2.

shirtless to display his
pumped torso and arms
tattoos exposed to the
sharp afternoon light
he stalks across the

the clinic parking lot
baseball cap on backwards
black kilt swaying with the
movement of his bare legs
sporran bouncing lightly
as he strides toward the door
daring anyone to say anything

LUCKY BOYS

Those boys in my
Catholic elementary school,
the ones who
beat me up
and called me
sissy,
fairy,
faggot,
how did they know about me
when I didn't even know
about myself?
Or was it just that they
were calling me the
worst names
they could think of,

and they got lucky?

KILLING THE QUEER

(in memoriam, Louis Pearson, murdered 05/02/1998)

They shoved a stick
up his nose into his brain.

The newspaper felt that we
needed to know that detail.

All the way into his brain.

And they beat him, of course,
the three of them beat him.
The pathologist found cause
of death to be 'blunt force
trauma to the head and neck.'

They left his body lying
down an embankment
at the edge of an orchard,
on the north end of Lake Mendocino.
His car was parked nearby.

These three brave young men
killed one lonely queer
then bragged about it
to their girlfriends, one
of whom turned them in.

They didn't just
beat him to death.

They shoved a stick
up his nose
into his brain
and, yes,
we do need to
remember
that detail.

BRAND LOYALTY

He told me that when they
moved into the dead man's
cabin up on Gardner Ridge,
way the hell out of town,
the de facto shelves of the
open 2x4s of the inside walls
were lined with empty
Old Overholt bottles.
Not a Jack Daniels, Jim Beam,
or I.W. Harper in sight,
just Old Overholt.
Years' worth, decades' worth.
Displayed all around the
old guy's cabin like the antidote
to a grandmother's collection
of Hummel figurines.

Such sustaining brand loyalty
impressed me and the next time
I was in the State Store I asked
for a bottle of the stuff to find
out what the old guy saw in it.
Even though I was a bourbon man,
I was not disappointed.
That rye was warm and went down like
fine sandpaper buffing a redwood burl.
While I wasn't about to give up

my bourbon, I could definitely
see the old guy's point, so
I dedicated that bottle to him.
And all the ones that followed.

SWEET COFFEE MORNINGS (1984)

On most mornings that year up
in the mountains Dan and I would
mount our Honda 110's and
ride down the steep, pot-holed,
dirt road to Kenny and Annie's
for cups of Annie's sweet coffee,
a concoction of basic Folgers
to which she added milk, sugar,
and generous whiskey.

During cold, rainy weather we'd
sit around the wood stove in the cabin.
When the season lightened we'd be
under the trees at the picnic table
savoring the lingering cool of night
before the sweltering day could begin.

I prefer my coffee black and strong
but I made exception for those
creamy delights, drinking them eagerly
before starting off on our daily rounds
of the patches, checking the plants on
which we were gambling our futures.

THE COOK AFTER CLOSING (1989)

ever notice the tendency to drink among cooks in general

– Neal Cassady, *The First Third*

Once everything is broken down,
lights lowered, kitchen quiet,
he goes to the corner of the bar
where lost shadows gather,
commandeers his usual seat,
pulls out a pack of cigarettes.
He smells of grease and sweat.
Bartender Tom brings his bourbon,
they exchange some words.
Someone tries to chat him up
but the cook is barely responsive,
until he gets a few drinks in him,
then he plugs old Motown
into the jukebox and babbles
to anyone pretending to listen.
If unapproached, he'll sit quiet,
smoking, sifting through ghosts
and unrealized expectations,
until Tom shuts the place down.

Then he walks to his rented home.
A two-liter bottle of cheap whiskey
sits next to his easy chair waiting for
him and a tumbler full of ice cubes.
He watches whatever's on cable,
chain smokes, lets his poisons
work their magic until he passes out.

He awakens three or four hours later,
ice melted, ashtray overflowing,
TV still the only light in the room,
the rude dawn has yet to arrive.
He gets fresh ice, starts over again.
The scent of saltwater mist from
Humboldt Bay, bittersweet in the air,
hides beneath the stench of cigarettes.
Sometimes he scribbles words
into a notebook, but mostly he just
kills his time until the next shift.

DAYBREAK

dawn's light seeps through
this grey layer of marine mist

the way blood seeps through
the gauze covering a wound

and the day threatens to break
across its hangover morning

like a full bottle of Tennessee
bourbon shattering against a rock

FIRST NIGHT IN DETOX

Everybody's got to have somebody to look down on.

– Kris Kristofferson

The junkie and the drunk
sat on opposite sides of
a small table in the
seen-better-days kitchen
of the detox house;
dripping faucet,
buckling linoleum floor.
Fighting off the shakes,
leaning into each other
across the table,
oozing menace,
rocks glasses of lemonade
close at hand,
arguing,
arguing:

at least I ain't no fucking drunk
yeah, well at least I ain't no fucking junkie
yeah, well at least I ain't no fucking drunk
yeah, well at least I ain't no fucking junkie

Over and over,
back and forth across
that kitchen table, which
seemed to shrink

a little bit more with
each slurred assertion,
for at least half that
endless fucking night.

DETOX
(April, 1990)

1.
I was already
drunk when
I got the call
at 7 AM
telling me
there was a
bed open
in detox
if I could be
there by 8

I knew I'd die
if I kept drinking
I knew I'd die
if I stopped
so what the fuck?
why not?

I dumped out bottles,
after farewell swallows
packed a bag with
underwear, toothbrush,
and cigarettes.

At 7:55 AM I
parked my truck
in front of an

ordinary, old
two-story house
in town,
broke the seal
on an airplane bottle
of Courvoisier,
downed it in one gulp,
tossed the empty
behind the seat, and
headed for detox.

2.
Three days of
rubber mattress,
rationed cigarettes,
ill-fitting pajamas,
floppy slippers and
shaky vital signs.

Three days of
drunks and
junkies
all jonesing
at once.

Three days of
meetings
counselors
groups

conferences held
almost
out of earshot

Three days of
weak lemonade
out of a huge jug

Three days of
late night TV
in a room full
of sweating
panicked people
feet twitching
cigarettes tapping staccato
against the edges of
plastic ashtrays

Three nights of
restless sleep
spilling into
early mornings
no appetite
dry mouth
filled with
hot smoke

3.
Then the shaking stops
the sweat dries
taken to a meeting
outside the house
for the first time
can't say the words
yet they let me ride
with the knowing
and after three days
I'm unceremoniously
dumped back
into the world
to return to my
job cooking
in a bar.

Explaining to
the bartender
where I've been.

Rearranging all
the furniture in
my house so nothing
is where it was before
when I reach
for the bottle
there isn't even
a place for it to rest.

For weeks every night
after closing up
the kitchen,
going back
to that detox
house to watch
late night TV
and chain-smoke
with the newbies
until being sober
became as normal
as it's ever
going to get.

PART II

Sleeping with fireflies

SLEEPING WITH FIREFLIES

Lightning bugs won't bite you,
nor do they sting,
nor do they crawl around
on your arm when you're
trying to eat a hot dog fresh
off a stick held over a campfire.
They do not dive bomb your ear, and
they don't go all kamikaze in your soda.

They just fly around in their own
little self-determined patterns
flirting with each other in
firefly semaphore,
bestowing magic on the muggy darkness,
meaning no one any harm
and no one means them any harm.

Even the children, who naively
capture them in peanut butter jars
washed out for just this purpose
with holes punched in the lid
and freshly pulled grass in the bottom,
mean them no harm. They are simply
enthralled with the wonder
of bioluminescence during twilight,
of the firefly in the summer night,
and they want to hold onto it,

set it next to their beds when
it is time to sleep, a nightlight,
a talisman, a way to bring magic
into the house, into their dreams.

DRY LIGHTNING

Coming off winter drought, when rain was a stranger,
fleeing, ignoring the needs of the land. Parched trees.

A hot wind rustles dry grass beneath triple digit oppression.
The sun bakes the exposed dirt of the orchard into dust.

Fans stir stagnant air failing to conjure the breeze
rising from the surface of a cold sea or the cool of night.

Sheriff's warning, dry lightning expected along the night coast.
Wherever it strikes potential fires erupt before surging winds.

A firetruck, siren pleading, races down this narrow
Road past my driveway toward a most rational fear.

DISSATISFACTION

Two owls
in the final
moments
of night,
their gullets
not yet
satisfied,
chatter on
to each other
protesting
the coming
dawn,
prepared to
argue
with the
sun itself, if
necessary.
That is,
until it
rises on
their
indignant
entreaties for
more time
to hunt
and they
fall
silent
into the
blinding
day.

SATISFACTION

Two owls
in the final
moments
of night,
their gullets
satisfied,
bellies full,
brag on
to each other
about their
kills, their
hunting skills
while
the coming
dawn,
fed up
already
with their
boasting,
prepares to
shut them
down with
sunlight,
to stop
their braggart
swaggering
and allow

the birds of
morning
to sing
into the
blinding
day.

BEFORE I WAKE

Insecure venetian blinds
Sweet unknowing of sleep
Comfortable illogic of dreams
Shed like a protective shell

Waking, raw, vulnerable
Awareness rushing back in,
Like a black Friday shopping mob
When the store doors open

In the half light of morning
Birds let each other know they
Made it through another night
I stir, wondering whether I have

AN ABSENCE OF SNOW

It doesn't snow here, although there
Are winter mornings when the frost
Is enough to make one wonder,
Joints grind against themselves,
Skin shudders, shedding warmth.

It does not snow here, though all the
Leaves have vacated their perches
And the naked branches hang empty
Anticipating the wet weight of snow,
Even though it won't snow here.

The calendar can tell me when winter
Has arrived or my bones can tell me,
Or the aches in muscles which never
Ached before when doing those things
Which no longer seem worth doing.

Bones know better than digital clocks,
Better than daylight savings time,
Better than the holiday displays in
Every store and on every downtown
Street where merchants ply their trade.

Snow has no power on the California
Coast, it is merely a distant relative
Who lives up in the boonies, sufficiently
Inclined to deep suspicion of outsiders
As to greet all visitors with a shotgun.

HUMMINGBIRD AT THE BOTTLEBRUSH

How do a hummingbird's wings
sound to the hummingbird?

Are they so loud that they drown
out the other sounds of the world?

Or does the hummingbird not
even hear them anymore, the

way a man grows accustomed
to the constant tinnitus of these

complicated times and learns to
hear only what he wants to hear.

BOBCAT

Under an
orange sun
bobcat drinks
from water
set out for deer
stalks a squirrel
across the yard
chases it halfway
up an oak tree
then changes his
mind and turns
around to climb
down head first
sits at the base
unsatisfied
still hungry for
blood and meat
the hunt and kill
while the squirrel
twitters on its
rocking branch
surviving for
one more day
of gathering
ripe acorns
and waiting
for rain.

PART III

Snapshots from a pandemic

HOW TO PLAY DEAD IN A PANDEMIC

1.
First, if you go out into the
world treat it like a camping
trip to the wilderness and
leave no trace. Then take nothing
with you when you return,
not so much as a pine cone,
a pretty stone, a microbe.

2.
Can we let lamb's blood simply be
a metaphor? Or do I actually have
to go out and kill a lamb to keep
plague away from my house? And,
if so, may I then share the lamb's
blood with friends and neighbors?
Or must we each kill our own?
And, with market shelves showing
the strain, can we then eat the lamb?
Or must it be burnt as an offering
to the god of one's choosing?

3.
A man lying low
turns the stereo down,
leaves the TV off,
paces the hallway
in slippers,
checks his temperature,

unlocks his car but
doesn't drive it,
considers symptoms,
rations his xanex,
washes his hands while
counting alligators.

MAGIC

With Ganesh above the entrance
and a mezuzah on the door jamb,
do I have enough magic to ward
an evil virus away from my home?

Do I need a crucifix? A pentagram?
What suggestions have you?
Three witches with a cauldron?
Buddhists chanting mantras?

Or just latex gloves and N-95s?
And where can I get those?
Tell me, quick!
I feel symptoms coming on.

ON THE TRAIL

Dogs snarl at each other
One barks "Six feet!"
The other barks back
"Where's your mask?"
They strain at the leashes
Of civilized society and
The leashes stretch taut
Ready to snap at any time.

HOUR OF THE WOLF

Awake at 3 AM to cold silence.
No music to disturb the night,
to let the wolf know I am about.
But the light gives me away,
now he sits, slavering, grunting
just outside the window where
I write. Crouching on the fresh
stump of a giant oak tree which
used to stand tall in that spot,
which used to creak and pop
when the wind blew strong,
unlike this quiescent morning
when nothing stirs but the wolf.
He wants into my house, tries to
sneak in on the soles of my shoes,
the surface of my hands. He wants
to settle down in front of my
heater, he wants food and drink
served to him. He wants my life.
The pack has been wandering,
hunting, sniffing out weakness,
stubbornness, sloppiness, the
slip-up and slipshod, those like me
who are overwhelmed by all the
precautions, warnings, admonitions.
Weary of the constant vigilance, of
being perpetually reminded that
the wolf is prepared to pounce
and we are supposed to be ready.

WASTED DAYS

Eating past hunger, contours expanding, thickening.
Emotions pushing appetite beyond need.

Time drags through the minutes, steeplechases
across days, weeks. Staggers into hazy dawns.

Jealous of hours spent sleeping, but worthless without them,
he fights it at night, clings to it in the morning.

Looking at books without reading them. Savoring titles,
nodding at authors like old friends seen across the street.

Distancing on the social apps. Gossip and politics.
Outrage exhaustion. No need to think for one's self.

Listening to Miles Davis from 1974. Daydreaming
about doing things that aren't a waste of time.

IN A SHOWER OF METEORS

Stars fall across the sky all night, the
flaming wonders of The Lyrid cluster
passing through his dreams. This
old man, too tired and cold to spend
half the night lying on the dew wet
grass staring at a splintering universe,
instead curls up in bed, aware of what
he cannot see from under his quilt.
He stays warm, safe, while knowing
he is waiving his chances for wishes.

There are other things he cannot see
burning through the night, seeping
into the day. The virus waits around
every gesture, on every surface,
travels on the breath of strangers,
leaps across too close distances like
a toad's tongue grasping at flies.

He fidgets with the idea of going out,
tucks it into his back pocket like a
paperback he intends to read someday,
decides to stay put where he is,
having determined that he has
enough diseases already and even
a shower of falling star wishes
won't make any of them go away.

WORKING FROM HOME

The house has grown tired of
having me around all the time.
It generates sour odors,
thickens stagnant air with humidity,
lays out electrical cords and
bunched up rugs in my path.
It doesn't care how often
I go out to walk around the yard,
it always grumbles when I return.
It wants its days back, its peace.
I have been in the way too long
with no sure sign of moving on.

RUSSIAN ROULETTE

It's playing Russian roulette with my mind.

– Van Morrison

High definition television images:
The middle-aged man in ICU
Tubes in his arms
Ventilator down his throat
Eyes half shut, unresponsive
Doctors and nurses masked
Behind shields within hazmat suits
Standing over him
They need that ventilator
Elsewhere

At the pharmacy old man
Bent over his canes
Coughs and hacks, no mask
Turns, leaves as I do
Holding the door for him
He calls out to a car
"I gotta wear a mask"
Like it's a surprise

Every venture out among
People strikes alarms
Which linger long after
Returning to safe isolation
But I keep going out anyway -
What IS the gestation period?

Anxiety turns back upon itself
Multiplies exponentially
Spinning through my gut
To my mind a dizzy fog
Of incomprehension
Pandemic panic added
To every other anxiety about
Life which never went away.

IN A TIME OF SURGES

We were throwing time away

               – Pere Ubu

The vineyard turns yellow, then brown
Oak and apple leaves cover the ground

Acorns roll along a corrugated
Sheet metal roof to leap off the edge

The starless overcast night gives way to
A grey day of indistinguishable shadow

Squirrels and deer root through
Dead leaves for ripened acorns

Wind and rain tease drought-twisted land
With a limp-wristed promise of relief

The man sits at his desk in his sleeping
Clothes well into the stark afternoon

He stares out the window into the empty
Middle distance between house and tree line

Mind hazy and slow as the morning weather
Thoughts indistinct and unproductive

Empty minutes morphing into hours, into days
Abstract as viral statistics in media reality

Life fading into the speculative fiction people
Cringe over and refer to as interesting times

Raindrops knock more leaves out of trees
The wind whirligigs them through the air

SNAPSHOTS FROM A PANDEMIC

Pacing the yard just past dawn. Birds chattering,
free to fly wherever they wish.

Television talking heads spewing numbers,
pointing to charts, which somehow translate into lives.

Mask as fashion statement. Sequined mask. Flag mask.
Mask as political position. Frightened old masked man.

What are your symptoms this morning? What?
You don't have any? Look again. Look again.

Talking to shadows. The empty guest chair.
The solitary bed. Swapping photos with Onan.

Even the recluse gets lonely when he's
denied what he had chosen to forego.

PART IV
Death stalking

THE BLACK HOOD

after "The Hangman's Poor Gift" by Philip F. Clark

When they place that black hood
over the head of the one to be
executed do they use a fresh one

each time or is it the same hood
used for all the others?
Do they wash it between, or can

the one about to die smell and
taste the last breaths of the ones
who came before?

DEATH STALKING

Of course death is stalking you
that's what death does to aging men,
what did you think he did?
Hang out at a crossroads waiting
for you to have a flat tire?
Did you think he would just
hide out, leave you alone,
until you call to him for relief?
You are death's road
and he will stay on it.
Friends and acquaintances
pass on without you. As each one
goes you feel as though they held
some lesson for you to learn.
But what have you learned?
Look around, who's left?
Your turn draws closer with each
hour spent idle, each day shuttered
with indifference, each year drifting
away, a trail of smoke wavering off
the wick of an extinguished candle.
Night growing unbelievably darker.

MY FATHER GOES TO FLORIDA (1978)

Midsummer on a Florida beach, wading into the moonlit
   glow of
the Atlantic, water erupts with leaping fish, shimmering
   shark food.

In the cardio ICU my father, hooked up to tubes and wires,
   sees me
enter and quietly starts to cry, realizing the family has been
   called.

He tells me he loves me and it is the only time I can remember
him ever saying those words; I don't know how to respond.

In the RV park insects hum in the darkness, televisions
mumble incoherently within mobile replications of home.

The only other time I saw my father cry was 1964. I was 11.
He was on the phone. Someone told him that his father died.

In a phone booth on a night muggier than Ohio a rainbow
   scarab
appeared, nearly as large as a praying mantis; metallic reflections.

MY FATHER RETURNS HOME (1978)

Released from the Florida ICU to the RV park, my father
teaches my mother how to pull a trailer all the way to Ohio.

I go back to my old restaurant job and wait for the phone to
ring from somewhere along the road toward Cleveland.

Home after many days of travel, and having abruptly quit both
cigarettes and beer, my father languishes, waiting for surgery.

The August days cool at night, but not enough. My brothers are
much younger but still too old for catching lightning bugs in jars.

Briefly alone one morning, a heart attack seizes him again,
lays him out on the kitchen floor for my mother to find.

The hospital tells me nothing except my mother wants me.
Once there, I see her through a glass wall, crying with a priest.

MY FATHER IS LAID TO REST

(1930-1978)

The wake was delayed to allow out-of-town friends and
relatives to make the trip, extending the raw pain for days.

Gently talking my mother and sister out of the expense of
an ornate, silk-lined casket and into one more reasonable.

The house full of grievers all the time, family I hadn't
seen since childhood and people I'd never met before.

Suited, at the funeral parlor door, greeting arrivals. Learning
   that
he proudly told co-workers his eldest son was a well-traveled
   poet.

My mother refused to leave for the funeral until I swallowed
one of the valium the doctor gave her for just that purpose.

Cemetery rain on the burial service. Hearing an aunt tell
my mother it means heaven is opening to let Johnny in.

MY MOTHER EXPRESSES REGRET (1979)

After my father died, leaving my mother with two teenaged
boys to raise alone, I stuck around for a bit to try to help.

We developed this habit of talking in the stairwell
each night when I got home from drinking at Baron's.

The kids would be in bed at last and she would tell me
about their day, her day, and sometimes talk about Dad.

One night she said to me, her eldest: *I hope I do better with
these two, because I sure blew it with the first two.*

She forgot who she was talking to. Though I knew exactly what
she meant, I responded: *I consider myself a screaming success.*

From within her reverie she snapped to, smiled awkwardly,
embarrassed for a moment, before continuing as before.

40 YEARS

My father's hat hangs
from the rack
on the landing
near the back door,
never once moved
in the 40 years
since he was
carried out that door
by paramedics.

Collecting layers of dust,
                    fading
in sideways sunlight,
gradually changing color,
never used anymore
                    by anyone.
Waiting for a dead man to
                    grab it on
his hurried way out the door
Waiting for my aging mother
                    to die
so it can finally be moved
before the house is sold.

Until then it hangs there
waiting for him to return.

MY MOTHER GROWS OLD

(1931-2019)

She hardly ever left the recliner but only rarely reclined it.
Gathered an afghan around her most of the time, always
    cold.

Grand and great-grandchildren visited occasionally.
    She told
me, "I can't believe I have a son who qualifies for MediCare."

The television was on all day as she nodded in and out.
    News, talk
shows, game shows, more news, police procedurals and
    sitcoms.

Memories of Santo Domingo, Las Vegas, Nashville Fan
Weeks, and the Knoxville World's Fair weighed on her
    static existence.

Several times every day she had to enter the kitchen to
    fix her
shrinking meals. Her husband died there four decades
    earlier.

The rugs were removed from her house to prevent
    another fall.
She stopped taking all her pills and then sat alone,
    waiting.

HOLY CARD

I met my mother's body
at a funeral home and
left with a holy card

the line of cars behind
the hearse in slow procession
along suburban streets

cemetery grit caught
under my fingernails
rust in my mouth

LIGHTNING WITHIN

inside vast towering clouds
lightning erupts sharp, arcing,
illuminating massive ethereal bulk
as though concealing tesla coils
deep within their wet recesses
the nervous electric flashes
of a mad scientist's laboratory
in a black and white horror
film flickering out of the 1930s –
we fly west, level with heaven,
as though we were equals -

behind me and far below
my mother is finally in
the ground next to my father
after waiting over 40 years
to have a date carved in stone
she joins him in death at last
having been the devoted,
loyal widow the whole time
mourning him longer
than she ever had him -

outside the airliner window
the lightning doesn't stop
it keeps cracking the sky
we simply fly past it
racing the sunset west
set from the start to lose

FOR JOHN, ON THE ANNIVERSARY
OF HIS SUICIDE

People still ask me why you did it, as though I might
   actually
have an answer simply because we were boyfriends for
   a while.

Sometimes someone will look at me, when speaking
of you, and openly wonder what you and I ever had in
   common. Me too.

Periodically you would call to tell me you were going
   to hang
yourself. I pointed out each time that your ceiling was
   too low.

Most of the plants you brought to my yard died soon
   after. The
wisteria, however, survives and becomes more invasive
   each year.

I have developed an answer to that question. Now I
   tell people:
John was profoundly disappointed with his life. That's
   all.

LOST AT SEA

The day that Jake, her commercial
fisherman fiancé, drowned, Connie came
in to work the dinner shift, as usual.
There were no wisecracks though and
she saved her smiles for the customers.
She handed orders to the cook without
comment. Picked them up the same.
She shrugged off condolences,
dismissed offers of help, and
cried quietly in the storeroom when
she thought no one was around.

In the early morning hours
the small boat Jake crewed on,
overloaded with a good catch,
capsized in rough seas just off the bar.
The captain and the one other crewmember
survived. Jake's body was never found.

That night, after her last table had been set,
Connie swept her tips into her purse,
without counting them, and left.

GRIEF IS A STRANGE CRITTER

with rough wiry hair and
blunted, curving claws.
He slinks around the edges
of the yard, whining, watching
through his narrow eyes.
Knowing he's been seen, he
still won't come out of hiding.
But when you're alone,
sitting in your easy chair,
he slips in the back door
to curl up at your feet.
In time you nod off.
When you wake,
he's in your lap,
warm, comfortable,
settled.

SHAUNA DIES REPEATEDLY

Walking on a hot day, stalking
shade from shadow to shadow,
I pass a lone man pacing
under the sparse branches
of a slender city tree
talking on his cell phone.

You know, to me
Shauna dies repeatedly
every day.

What he says next is lost as I keep walking
but now I'm wondering, who is Shauna?
Girlfriend? Wife? Daughter?
And how did she die?
If she is really dead, or
is she just dead to him or
does he just wish she were dead?
How does she die repeatedly
and why does this happen every day?
Was he responsible for her death?
Was he driving the car that crashed?
Did he provide the drugs she ODed on?
Did she commit suicide over his infidelity?
Or was the infidelity hers?

WHAT HAPPENED TO SHAUNA??

I try to remember his tone when he said it.
Was he sad? Angry? Hurt? Matter-of-fact?

It escapes me, it happened too fast.
I put spin after spin on it but nothing satisfies.
There is no resolution to the Shauna problem.
She haunts each step for the rest of my walk
as she keeps dying repeatedly the whole way.

AFTERLIFE

to Jim Lang

I try to convince myself
there is an afterlife
so I can see you again.
So I can listen to you
talk of art and music
Wittgenstein and Barthes.
So we can walk the galleries
of the CMA together.
Listen to Karel Paukert play
Messiaen and Bach on
the McMyler Memorial Organ.
Then we'll head west to Baron's
for cheap shots and
big fishbowls of cold beer.
And where you can explain
to me again about SEAL:
The Society for the Elimination
of Adagios and Largos.
Could Baron's have
an afterlife, too?
Is that too much
to ask of religion?
A heaven for bars? Why
not believe in such a heaven?
A place where you occasionally
wonder when I will arrive.
I'm not far now.
It won't be long.

Which religion
would guarantee me
such a heaven?
Sign me up for it.
Baptize me in the
blood of the blue moon.
Drill me in the rituals.
Sell me the holy book.
My devotion will be pure.
My tithing, perfect.

EVEN STARS DIE

(after "Bon Vivre" by Alfred Starr Hamilton)

Nestled in the black night,
elegant as diamonds in a
jewelry store display case,
galaxies of stars gaze back at us,
bewildered and impotent.

They watch us stumble through
insignificant lives on this
insignificant ball of dust where
even the best livers don't live
forever. Like the stars, which

eventually either explode into
supernova or fade away, burning
into a cinder, drifting aimless
through the immensity of space,
while men debate immortality.

PART V
The old fart takes a header

THE RELATIVE SANCTITY OF OBJECTS

Pick up each thing, tell me the story, then we'll throw it away.

– John Cwiakala

Memories alive as spirits encased in objects,
Set in amber, locked in lucite, wrapped in plaster,
Hanging within webs of spider and silk worm.

A small shell, butterfly, baby shoes, decayed molar,
A coffee cup, refrigerator magnet, Limoges china,
That chair, that blanket, that framed photograph.

The bed which witnessed such tender gymnastics
Turned over to the junk man and thrown onto his truck.
Things given away, things thrown away, things kept.

A 1920s straight razor, a 1903 Colt .32 revolver.
Hoping to feel lighter when the gravity of the past
Still weighs heavy, tethered to dead men's things.

THOUGHTS ON ABANDONED BOOKS

(after Jeffrey Long's 2019 painting "Abandoned Books 2")

There is a warm pool of
books within which to
wade one's mind up to
the knees or as deep
as one might please.

They appear to have been
tossed together like tinder
at the feet of Joan of Arc,
the feet of witches and heretics
burned throughout the ages.

They present a hazardous situation,
attempting to climb this
literary scree could send one
sliding backward down the
mountainside of ideology.

Or they could be leaves, these books,
raked into a pile on a chilly autumn day,
children jumping into them
before they are set aflame,
wafting as smoke into the sky.

My inner librarian wants to
gather them like stray livestock,
corral them alphabetically,
each within an appropriate category
then walk away, satisfied.

The abandoned books have bled
their words into the air, content
evaporated into atmosphere,
desiccated blank page carcasses left
behind for a frustrated bibliophage.

Eventually the lost words will
rain down on us in a new order
in some uncertain future
where words might yet be allowed
to carry untrammeled truth.

ENDSHEET

On the last blank page of a used, mail-order
paperback I find a careful pencil drawing of two
people, a man and a woman, seen from behind in
an airplane or bus.

The man is seated on the aisle, his short sleeve
reveals tattoos rendered in fine detail. He holds a
cell phone in that hand. There is a chain from his
back pocket to his belt loop, each link distinct.

There is less to see of the woman, the side of her
head, a dangling earing. The only feature visible
on her face is a small mole midway between her
invisible eye and her ear. She, too, holds a cell
phone.

The artist captured her mole, the stubble on the
man's cheek, hints at a border between hair and
hat, differentiating without defining, allowing
ambiguity a chance to undermine presumption.

SOME RANDOM THOUGHTS

(after "My Favorite Houseguest" by Mike James)

Gertrude Stein

In Paris I ate in a restaurant where she and Alice took Samuel Stewart when he would visit them. A wall of mirrors, echoes. Small stones cover her grave at Pere Lachaise and a jar of pens.

Bette Davis

She brought a dignity to *Baby Jane* that Joan Crawford could never muster, though she might have thought she could. I love her best when she is being bad, but still keep watching *All About Eve*.

Self-Portrait, In Movies

They're all Swedish.

Andy Kaufman

Fascinated me, but never sure why. I watched him whenever the chance arose. He was hairy, which always gets my attention, but I would not have had a beer with him. He'd have squished this bug.

Marilyn Monroe

She died just before I turned 10 but even I knew about the pills. I loved her from *Monkey Business* and *River of No Return*. She's my Diva, her sadness kisses the world. Bright red lipstick.

Orson Welles

Brilliance is not enough. One is required by success
to learn compromise, absent which creation become
difficult. Not impossible, but difficult and costly to
both body and soul

J.R. Ewing

I could never get over expecting Jeannie to appear at
some inconvenient time in the drama. Or thinking
about his mother flying around a stage on wires,
pretending to be a young boy.

Billy Strayhorn

Always in shadow, that is where his type had to live
then. The shadow beneath Duke's piano, the shadows
of alleys and bushes after closing time. Today he'd be a
star casting his own shadows.

Steve McQueen

Sullen and sexy. Eventually sullen won out. Whether
riding a motorcycle or a horse he always seemed in
cold control. In the living room he feels impatient, not
really wanting to be there.

Sal Mineo

I knew he had the hots for Dean, everyone knew that,
but I couldn't say it. Dean knew too, and didn't send
him away. Somehow that made it OK for me to feel it,
but still not say it.

John Wayne

(for Jason Baldinger)

He had his shtick, repeating it in nearly every film.
John Ford knew what to do with him the same way

he knew how to use Monument Valley. Marion was
always watching, just off-camera.

Nixon

Throwing Agnew under the wheels didn't help.
Nor the secret plan to end the war. Nor did China.
Checkers. Sweltering under studio lights. From out of
his ashes emerged government as a business.

Warren Zevon

The world twists in ways we seldom anticipate but
with which he seemed intimate. His songs charted for
other people, which kept checks coming in until his
shit got fucked up and he checked out.

John Ritter

I had a crush on him but hated that sitcom character:
straight actor playing a straight man mincing around
as gay for cheap rent. I'd watch occasionally, hoping
he'd take his shirt off. Never saw it.

David Wojnarowicz

Played rough along the edges of American culture
and America played back, rougher. Waterfronts, alleys,
aging sleazy movie houses, backrooms. Broken
streetlights in the urban world night.

Lou Reed

A belligerent interviewee, he took no prisoners. Knew
Delmore Schwartz. Married Laurie Anderson and
started meditating. Died when even his transplanted
liver gave up. The music. The music.

TEN MOVIES

(after Tim Dlugos)

Niagara (1953)

Marilyn sings along, breathlessly, with a record.
Can't remember why she married Joseph Cotton.
Jean Peters studies the way she moves.

The Ten Commandments (1956)

Everything pales before the parting of the Red Sea,
its walls collapsing onto Pharaoh's charioteers.
Piety and the wisdom of masculine flesh.

Cries and Whispers (1972)

Sisters gather for the death of the spinster.
The nursemaid gives the dying woman her breast.
The husbands are oblivious.

Barb Wire (1996)

Pamela playing Bogie playing Rick
in a gender role bending dystopia.
Don't call me babe.

Island of Lost Souls (1932)

Family values moralist encounters mad
scientist who only wants to be left alone.
We may not all be men after all.

The Cooler (2003)

Limping schlub falls in love with waitress
in the casino where they both work.
Everyone gets just what they deserve.

The Monolith Monsters (1957)

Space crystals multiply, grow gigantic,
collapse onto buildings, turn people to stone.
Just add water.

The Conversation (1974)

Somebody is listening to everything.
Gene Hackman playing saxophone in
the twilit apartment he's just torn apart.

Quintet (1979)

Everybody's breath is visible.
Dogs eat corpses in a frozen city.
Paul Newman's ice blue eyes.

The Letter (1940)

Bette being a bad girl on a rubber plantation
while subjugated natives huddle in huts
waiting for the white men to kill each other.

FAMOUS
I want to be born a big diamond on the finger of Elizabeth Taylor.
> – Andy Warhol, in an interview with John Giorno

I met one of Andy Warhol's former lovers at a poetry reading.
He was sweaty, friendly, patient, and signed a book for me.

I once bumped into Allen Ginsberg as he was coming out
of a port-a-potty I needed to get into. We both apologized.

A friend of mine had been one of Robert Mapplethorpe's
    lovers.
When he speaks of the photographer his aging eyes still grin.

After talking with James Broughton for over twenty minutes
I came completely untethered from the bookstore floor.

When first I met Harry Hay we spoke for a while in an open
    field
then he kissed me, slipping his 85 year old tongue into my
    mouth.

I met Gregory Corso in a Gold Beach, Oregon bar. He called
    out to
each person who entered: *I'm a famous poet! Buy me a
    drink!*

THE OLD FART TAKES A HEADER

As far as the Old Fart could tell
it was a Grand Canyon of a fall,
in slow motion, ending before it
began, from an Everest of a curb
in the supermarket parking lot.

Formed concrete caught his shoe
with the sharpened nails of a
gremlin's claw and down he went;
a header, face first into wood chips.
Scuffed knees, bloody forehead.

Everything changes at that moment,
lying on moist ground in the day's
penumbra of mercury vapor lights,
life slips into a surreal mode where
nothing seems quite right anymore.

A stranger passing by pauses, shifts
his shopping bags, asks if he's ok.
The Old Fart, on auto-pilot and noting
that he's not yet dead, mumbles, *yeah*.
The young man continues on his way.

A fracture of the Axis vertebrae,
yes, sir! That's a broken neck! But he
doesn't know that yet and rolls over
onto his back, rocks to his side doing
the old fart boogie-woogie, he rises.

In the supermarket the lights are too
bright, everyone is staring at him,
the floor wavers like undulations in
the surface of a calm pond, just enough
to make him feel uneasy on his feet.

He pats with a handkerchief at the
blood running off his forehead,
stares into the restroom mirror,
splashes cold water on his face, the
blood dilutes but doesn't stop flowing.

The stunned Old Fart asks a checker for
a first aid kit and finds himself seated
on a bench with employees fawning
over him, bandaging his forehead,
giving him water he doesn't want.

It'll just make me pee, he tells her.
They offer to call an ambulance but
the Old Fart knows what that means
and takes to his feet, wobbly, to
venture out and finish his shopping.

Fuck them and their ambulance, he
mumbles as he wanders back and forth.
He repeats the same path, putting things
in his basket then taking them out again
until the confusion overwhelms him.

He hits the check-out line, pays in a haze,
stumbles out to his car and drives his ass
to the post office to check for mail. His
neck shooting electric shocks into his head,
into his shoulders. This might not be good.

Instead of heading home he hesitates, then
turns toward the nearby emergency room.
He parks, musters his mettle and walks inside
where he tells the woman he fell on his head.
Apologizes for taking her time for nothing.

Bored, she questions him until he reveals
he's on blood thinners. He is whisked off
down labyrinthine corridors in a wheelchair,
loosely tucked into a gap-back gown,
then lifted over onto a CT scanner table.

They are looking for blood on his brain.
Nothing is found there, but that fracture
turns up at C2 so the hustle does not abate
simply shifts focus from the brain to the
spine and now flexion/extension x-rays

are ordered, STAT. The dizzy Old Fart
does his best to stand still but wavers
in front of the machine as though the
floor were pitched at an uncomfortable,
unfamiliar angle, feet bereft of bone.

With the kindly x-ray tech's help he
does it at last before settling back in the
wheelchair for the ride down crowded halls
to the temporary sanctuary of the room
where his book and cell phone await him.

Then the too young doctor comes back, he
asks the Old Fart, when did he break his neck
before? Didn't he break his neck before?
The Old Fart stumbles around his past seeking
occasions for an unnoticed broken neck.

The fracture appears stable, but the surgeon
will decide that. Surgeon? When had they
mentioned surgery? How did he miss that?
They put him in a cervical collar, then
tell him he can get dressed and go home.

Without even a prescription for pain pills
he's been dismissed. Time to move on.
They need that bed. The nurse says goodbye
and suggests a joint after he gets home.
You do have a ride home, don't you?

In the parking lot the Old Fart pops a xanex
before getting behind the wheel to learn
just what this all means. He can't turn his
head side to side, can't look behind him.
driving is an anxiety generating adventure.

At home, after excavating expired Norco out
of the depths of the refrigerator, and while
undressing for the second time that evening,
he finds a large splinter of wood chip in his
pants pocket as though he needed evidence

beyond this contraption clutching at his
throat, circling his neck, perching on
his chest and back like the blunted talons
of a half-tamed predator and he, by process
of elimination, determined to be prey.

He waits to be carried away through the sky,
waits for the up side, an orchid rising out of
the dark fog he's fallen into from a parking lot
curb, this strange life of limitations he'd never
before considered, this freshly-minted reality.

M.J. (Michael Joseph) Arcangelini was born 1952 in western Pennsylvania, grew up there & in Cleveland, Ohio. He's resided in various parts of California since 1979, currently in Sonoma County. He began writing poetry at age 11. His work has been published in many print magazines and online journals (see Acknowledgements page) and over a dozen anthologies. He is the author of five previous poetry collections: the full length *With Fingers at the Tips of My Words,* 2002, from Beautiful Dreamer Press, the chapbooks *Room Enough,* 2016, and *Waiting for the Wind to Rise,* 2018, both from NightBallet Press, the full length *What the Night Keeps,* 2019, Stubborn Mule Press, and *A Quiet Ghost,,* 2020, Luchador Press. He maintains an occasional blog of primarily memoirs at https://joearky.wordpress.com/